Buc

Living a Life of Happiness, Mindfulness and Peace

2 -

Table of Contents

Introduction

There is a lot to be said for seeking a calmer way of life that allows you to find a little happiness. With the world at loggerheads and wars being fought in the name of religion, it's time to look inward and to find out what Buddhism is all about. You may not want to give up your modern way of life to embrace Buddhism, but the joy of Buddhism is that you don't have to. Elements of Buddhism can be incorporated into your life because it's more a philosophy than a religion. This book is for those who are seeking a way forward that embraces happiness, and shows you how you can achieve that, using Buddhist philosophy as your guide.

You may have seen the Dalai Lama on TV or on YouTube videos and if you haven't then perhaps it is time that you did. He is the current leader of Buddhism though there are many branches of this type of thought and philosophy. Our book, however, goes back to the roots and tells you how Buddhism came about and what it means in this day and age. When you are able to embrace some of the teachings, you will find that it will bring you much happiness, peace and awareness – both of self and of others. This, in turn, leads to a kind of enlightenment that I am proud to have.

The reason for wanting to share this with you is because it is so simple to incorporate into your life if you want to. All you need is the ability to become mindful and when you do, it changes everything. I remember, a long time ago, wondering where I would find happiness. Everything around me seemed to be filled with stories of sorrow. I didn't know where to find comfort or joy. Many people in the world today are faced with similar stories. However, my journey into Buddhism was something that I have never regretted and it has become a mainstay for my life and can be for yours.

Perhaps you have tried other things such as yoga and meditation and failed. However, when you put things into perfect perspective and embrace the ideas that were thought up by the original Buddha, you begin to see things in a much different way and are less critical of others, learn humility and can piece all the pieces together that were otherwise scattered to the winds. How? That's where this book comes in. We will take you through the history, so that you can easily make sense of Buddhism and then we will take you through the different things that you can do to embrace it and make it part of your life. Does it matter what religion you are? Not at all. Buddhism is philosophy. Thus, a Christian can practice it just as easily as someone from another religion. Take this journey of discovery and see for yourself what's in it for you and how it can enrich your life.

The idea of this book is to help you to see how you can incorporate Buddhist philosophy into your life. It takes you on a journey where you learn where Buddhism comes from the some of the practices that it encompasses. You will see that you can incorporate some of these into your life and have very positive effects indeed, because all of the activities that we have suggested are positive ones which will help you to develop your own sense of spirituality and awareness.

We will also take you through what mindfulness is and touch upon meditation and breathing techniques that will help you on your journey. As you read through the book, you are encouraged to add aspects to your life, which you can very easily, without compromising whatever religion you believe in. Buddhism does not conflict with other beliefs. In fact, it celebrates them as much as you do. It's your personal choice that matters and Buddhism just helps you to get to the heart of your beliefs and make them stronger.

It takes who you are and makes it better and that can't be bad. If you are wondering how to incorporate some aspects of Buddhism into your lifestyle, then you have come to the right place because we understand that not everyone can devote their lives to a new philosophy. However, since this philosophy came about as the answer to the suffering of mankind in general, it is applicable to all who practice it and will help to improve their lives and lessen that suffering. It does not conflict with religious interests, so you can still follow your own religion and incorporate Buddhism at the same time. As stated previously, this is a philosophy or way of life and imposes nothing upon you that you do not see as beneficial to your life. The energy that you gain from Buddhist philosophy and the compassion that you learn to embrace will be worthwhile. The journey may be a short diversion for you to experience something new, but when you learn how simple it is to include Buddhism into your life, you may be surprised at how long term that journey becomes. Once learned, it's never forgotten and the moment that you tread off the path of Buddhism, your mind and body will know it and will point you back toward the direction you need to be going in. It's not forced. It's not ruled by a lot of impossible dogma. In fact, it makes very great sense and will enhance your life no end.

Chapter 1 – The Original Buddha

"We are shaped by our thoughts; we become what we think. When the mind is pure, joy follows like a shadow that never leaves."

~ Buddha

In case you are unfamiliar with the story of Buddhism, now is as good a time as any to introduce you to the idea of Buddhism. The original Buddha, Siddhartha Gautama, was a teacher and spiritual leader who lived 2500 years ago. That's a very long time, and the place in which he resided was Kapilavatthu, in India, which lay at the foothills of the Himalayas. He was not lowly by birth. In fact his father was a well-known King, King Suddhodana and his mother – Queen Maha Maya. One may ask therefore how someone with such a high position would have come up with the philosophy of Buddhism that seems so humble in its beliefs. However, the story is a simple one. Even back in those times, man was at odds with man. People were unhappy and what Siddhartha Gautama was looking for was a solution that would help people to attain happiness.

With parents who were well respected as fair leaders, Siddhartha Gautama was almost sure to become a Prince in his own right. However, when his mother died shortly after his birth, his father worried that Siddhartha would not wish to follow that pursuit, but that he would instead elect to be a monk, which was predicted when the name of the child was chosen by wise men. He learned as a child that happiness was something that all creatures and humans strive for. Brought up by the sister of his mother, Siddhartha was a very kind child and had respect for all living things. He could see that life was not that complex when looked at from a philosophical concept and learned that people derive happiness from being kind to others. Although this seemed simplistic, bear in mind that at the time, Siddhartha was still relatively young. He would not abide suffering of any kind and was kind to animals and to people in the same way because he found this to be the most natural way to find happiness and to embrace it as part of his life.

The King was unhappy to find that his son was contemplating deeply on the sadness and suffering in the world and ordered a palace to be built for his son, in an attempt to tempt his son to stay with him. He did not want to lose his son and thought that this distraction may make his son happier and less likely to be lost to a spiritual world spent in contemplation. In yet another attempt to keep his son from being lured into meditation and away from the life that his father had built for him, Siddhartha was to marry his cousin, Princess Yasodhara. Before a marriage could take place, it was traditional for a young man to prove himself worthy by taming a horse and Siddhartha took his own stance on this and tamed the horse with words and with kindness. He won the hand of his cousin because of the achievement.

As you can imagine, the Prince and his bride were offered a wonderful palace though this did not stop him from wanting to know what went on beyond the palace walls. When introduced to the outside world, Siddhartha was shocked to find that people get old. His life was surrounded with people who were relatively well off, and it was a shock to find that everyone lived a life and that they were all heading in the direction of old age and would eventually be like the men that he had seen outside the walls of the palace.

The pattern of events that shaped the life of Siddhartha led him to wanting to find a way where people would be able to avoid suffering. Even though his wife had given birth to a son, he still felt that he needed to leave the family palace and go out into the world to see what caused suffering. He was only 29 but what he had seen had tempted him to become a monk who would need to beg for food like other monks, depending upon the generosity of others. Learning about the sacrifice of animals, he taught people about the law of karma, which meant that if someone spread unhappiness, they would reap the same unhappiness. You may have heard of Karma and this plays a big part in Buddhism.

Study followed and although this took on the traditional way where a student and wise man work together, Siddhartha found that the knowledge that he had gained brought him no closer to understanding why people have to suffer. He further learned about meditation and it was meditation that took him to following the road toward Asceticism, which is where people deprived themselves of food and water because they believed that this would bring them to being repaid by being able to enter the kingdom of heaven. Saved from starvation, Siddhartha learned that this was perhaps not the way that he wanted to go. He wanted to find out what caused human suffering and going back to normal eating, but devoting his life to meditation, it was this meditation that led him to answers which are all encompassed in the Buddhist way of thinking. He believed that Buddhism was the way to end suffering. His enlightenment took him to a place that is known as "Nirvana" or that perfect happiness, and Buddhism is based upon his findings, which were placed into Truths that all Buddhists follow in their attempt to reach the same level of understanding. You need to know this, because without knowing where this philosophy comes from, you can't realize the significance of what the original Buddha discovered - much of it relevant to the way that Buddhists live their lives and find inner peace and happiness.

It may be worthwhile looking into the history from another perspective as well. By knowing why Buddhism was brought into being, you can see how it fits with your own ideology and much of the time, the feelings of Siddhartha are still feelings that people in this day and age experience. Thus, it follows that the solutions remain unchanged and that if you can find a way to incorporate those same answers into your life, you are likely to find the same peace that practicing Buddhists have found through following the rules that were put in place so long ago.

Following the teachings of the current Dalai Lama, it's easy to see how simplistic the views are and yet so many people fail to grasp them. The original Buddha's only intention, with the introduction of Buddhism's guidelines, was to ensure that people didn't have to go through all the suffering that he witnessed. His meditation paid off because he saw clearly that the happiness of mankind lay firmly in their own hands.

"Happiness is not something readymade. It comes from your own actions."

~ Dalai Lama

What the Dalai Lama is saying within this quotation spells out the simplicity of finding happiness. Even if you cannot embrace all of the ideology of Siddhartha, anything that you can incorporate is going to make your life happier and take away a level of suffering that you may otherwise find you live with through simply not knowing how to escape it. The study done by Siddhartha was not done in vain. Millions of people have found happiness through following the guidelines. Buddhist centers have been set up all over the world, but that doesn't count the people who, in their everyday lives, decide to follow some of the beliefs and also benefit as a direct result. This book is for them, those seeking truth and happiness and not quite ready to take the leap of faith into fully fledged Buddhism, though open minded enough to try to see how Buddhism may be fitted into their otherwise busy lives. It helps them to gain energy and to feel more compassion toward others, as well as being fulfilled in a truly spiritual sense. Join us on the journey and choose for yourself, because ultimately, the answer to your own happiness lies in your response to Buddhist philosophy and the incorporation of it into your everyday life.

Chapter 2 – The Four Noble Truths

"To enjoy good health, to bring true happiness to one's family, to bring peace to all, one must first discipline and control one's own mind. If a man can control his mind he can find the way to Enlightenment, and all wisdom and virtue will naturally come to him."

~ Buddha

The Four Noble Truths were discovered by Siddhartha Gautama during his search and consist of elements that are fairly easy to understand:

First Noble Truth – The Truth of Suffering

This is something that cannot be denied. Suffering exists. Each time you are tormented by mental or physical pain, suffering exists. This truth helps people to see that there is a universal truth that applies to everything in life. Suffering is real. Of course, everyone knows this to be true as they see things happening every day of their lives that they consider to be unfair or unjust. One needs only to turn on the television to see that people all over the world are indeed suffering.

The Second Noble Truth – The Truth of Cause of Suffering

Suffering doesn't just happen. There must always be a cause. Thus, if you tackle the cause, you are able to stem the suffering. Developing the mind to see things in a new way can help people to find the cause of suffering and that's half the battle of dealing with suffering. The cause of suffering may not always be apparent. It may be obscured, but it will always be there, lurking in the shadows. Buddhist philosophy is that one should not contribute to the cause of suffering for others. Indeed it is against the rules of Karma and would mean experiencing suffering as a direct consequences of such actions. Remember that in this day and age, it is easy to judge situations and often the wiser path is to observe rather than add to the injustice by judging those perceived to be at fault. There is no blame attached to the cause of suffering. It simply needs to be observed to be the truth. When blame rears its ugly head, it means more suffering because one is introducing a negative element into a positive life. Therefore, thought is necessary and this comes from meditation and from observation without judgment.

The Third Noble Truth – The Truth of the End of Suffering

Putting things simply, and simplicity works exceedingly well in Buddhism, if you know what the cause of the suffering is, you have more power in ending it. The biggest belief in Buddhism is that the Original Buddha reached that place called Nirvana and this is what Buddhists strive for because this is where suffering ends. Nirvana happens when you reach a certain level of understanding where you begin to see the truth. Many strive to get there, many get lost along the way.

The Fourth Noble Truth – The Truth of the Path Leading to the End of suffering

Buddhists are taught different pathways toward unleashing happiness and being able to rid themselves of suffering. The Eight Fold Path comes under this heading and this is where Buddhists are able to glean a better understanding of life and become happier. The eight fold path incorporates things that you can use to find happiness too. Right understanding, Right attitude, Right speech, Right Action, Right Livelihood, Right Effort, Right Mindfulness and Right Concentration are all part of the path that Buddhist Monks follow in order to reach enlightenment.

You don't need to understand these in great depth at this stage, but you can see from the above that your approach to life and to others, the way you make your living, the way you learn mindfulness and concentrate on becoming a better person all have a role to play in finding happiness. Thus, in future chapters, we will relate to this part of Buddhism and make it crystal clear how you can incorporate parts of the Buddhist philosophy to make your own life and the lives of those around you much more rewarding in a spiritual way.

Thus, what you need to learn, in a nutshell is how to develop your own understanding of life and behave in a certain way that brings you happiness, how to develop your mind and how to gain wisdom.

While you may feel that we have looked into this a little too heavily, believe me, we haven't. You just need to know where we are going and why when we advise you of ways that you can change your approach to life to embrace the Buddhist way. With the historical part over and done with, we can go on to explain how you can use and embrace Buddhism in your life, in this day and age, and end your own suffering, based on the study of the Original Buddha, whose philosophy has been proven to work. Even though all of the different rules of Buddhism were written 2500 years ago, they are still very relevant to today's world and will continue to be so. In the following chapters, we will show you how to incorporate the thinking of Siddhartha Gautama in your life, and thus see how Buddhism can make your life a much happier and more peaceful place to be. You will see, as I did, what Buddhism offers you and a lot of it is common sense, though we have perhaps evolved and thought ourselves too intelligent these days to follow the philosophy. Once you step back and see how modern life may just be standing in the way of your own happiness, you will be able to improve your life by using Buddhist philosophy and mindfulness into your life.

Mindfulness and the rules of Buddhism put together make you very aware of cause and effect. You are able to distinguish your own errors of judgment. You are also able to look with compassion at problems that are troubling you or others. You are able to find solutions, not through blame – but through careful deduction and inner thought. Buddhism is a way of life. It is not a religion. You may ask then why there are Buddhist monks and the reason is simple. These are the people who have chosen to follow Buddhist philosophy to the letter in order to find enlightenment that leads them to Nirvana. You, on the other hand, may come from any background or be of any nationality or religion, though you may still want to discover what truths the philosophy of Buddhism holds in store for you.

Buddhism can be practiced by anyone who chooses to practice it. The Four Noble Truths are as acceptable in one religion as much as in another. Thus, by having an understanding of them, you are able to make much more sense of life and begin to realize that all suffering comes as a direct consequence of human action and that human action can also lead one to release from that suffering. It makes sense to try to incorporate parts of the Buddhist philosophy into your life because, in doing so, you are naturally going to improve the way that you approach life and find truth that is simple to understand and to act on.

Chapter 3 – Incorporating Buddhist Philosophy into Your Life

"There are only two mistakes one can make along the road to truth; not going all the way, and not starting."

~ Buddha

My understanding of Buddhism took a while and it will be the same for you, until you get over the hurdle. You can't reach that hurdle if you don't actually start somewhere. It doesn't have to be religion. It doesn't have to be belief in any particular thing except yourself. You are the center of your universe, but that doesn't make you more important than others. Often, you hear people talking about how people have wronged them and sounding indignant because they feel that they are in the right and that people who have wronged them are in the wrong. It's a logical conclusion, but it isn't the only conclusion. Let me try and explain:

If you are hurt by something that someone does to you, your interpretation of what happens is what makes you decide upon who is at fault. You analyze, you are unhappy and feel betrayed and you step back into the situation so many times trying to find answers. Under the Buddhist way of looking at things, you wouldn't do that. What you would do is learn to live in the moment. When you learn meditation, you learn to be in that exact moment, rather than delving into the past or worrying about the future. That may sound a little idealistic, but it is and what's wrong with idealism? What you need to do before you are able to do this is to strip back all the layers of suppositions and see yourself for who you really are. That's the hard bit and I will explain how I did it because you can do this in just the same way.

Awe is what takes you there. If you know a place that awes you, then this is a wonderful place to start. My particular place was on the top of a hill overlooking moorland where I could look out on the world and feel very small indeed. I am small. I am one small grain of sand in reality. Why would you want to feel small? It brings you nearer to understanding creation and that's a good place to start to see Buddhist philosophy at its best. Just because you are small, that doesn't make you unimportant. A field of grass without one blade of grass is a different field of grass and if you are small you are still a part of the wonders of the Earth and creation and are part of something extremely special. If you know a place that awes you, go there. Close your eyes, think about nothing, and then open them. Make sure that when you do this, you empty your mind and are able to take in the beauty that you are surrounded with because this is part of understanding Buddhist philosophy. We know that we suffer. We know there are causes for suffering, but for one moment in time, we are going to step back from suffering and start to see ourselves for who we really are. Be awed. Breathe in the scenery because with that moment of awe comes a kind of renewal that you can't experience in your everyday life at this time. You will be able to, but first you need to recognize how small you are in the order of things. Once that is accepted, then all things are possible. On my hill, I felt humble. I felt a huge sense of humility and stripping back the layers of self-importance and seeing that humble character that lurks beneath the skin is vital to being able to grow spiritually.

To carry on from this, tell yourself that whatever has happened to you in the past is gone and that you have no control over the future. It is the now, the moment that you are in that is all that matters. That's what mindfulness will teach you. You will need to learn how to use

Buddhist Meditation because this helps you to put all the baggage from the past back into a place where it has less importance or significance and will be able to understand that the future moment is one that hasn't happened yet.

The current Dalai Lama has a very good quotation about the way that people pass their time and live and I think it's important to introduce this now so that you understand where this chapter is going. This was his answer when it came to being asked about where humanity goes wrong:

"Man. Because he sacrifices his health in order to make money. Then he sacrifices his money to recuperate his health. And then he is so anxious about the future that he does not enjoy the present; the result being that he does not live in the present or the future; he lives as though he is never going to die. And then dies having never really lived."

I love this quotation because the Dalai Lama kind of sums up what people are doing with their lives and the reason why so many people are unhappy. It took me a while to understand the full significance of what he was saying because I too was too wrapped up in my life to actually see the vicious circle I was letting my life get caught up in. We all do it, but we are all capable of learning to step off that roundabout and start to see life for the pleasure that it offers in every waking moment. That's what learning the Buddhist way will do for you. You will no longer hide behind the sins or regrets of the past. You will no longer be so concerned about the future – but you will be grounded in the NOW and in doing so, learn that you can achieve happiness and that this is the kind of happiness that brings inner peace and understanding that makes you a happier person. Thus, the first lesson is to work out the role that mindfulness plays in your life.

Over the next couple of chapters, we will take a look at step by step incorporation of Buddhist philosophy into your normal everyday life, so that you can begin to see the benefits. For someone who is unaccustomed to this philosophy, you will find that the chapters give practical ways in which you can make Buddhist philosophy part of your life and do this in a very common sense way, so that it isn't the framework of your life that needs to change. It is merely incorporating different elements of Buddhism and fitting them into your lifestyle. This is the part that many struggle with and my attempt in this book is to show you how, in practical terms, you can live your modern day life but using the values that were devised by Siddhartha as a means to put an end to your suffering and make your life happier.

When you see the prayer flags flying high against the blueness of the sky on a Tibetan mountain, you no longer question the validity of Buddhism. These prayer flags have been placed there by believers and the thoughts behind them reach out toward the heavens, just like your prayers do in whatever religion you follow. If you don't follow a religion, then that's quite acceptable too. Imagine those prayer flags in the same way as you imagine all kinds of good things when you see a child blow a bubble, or when you see the head of a dandelion be blown into the winds. It is merely the passage of a moment and one that you will grow to understand better, as you change your life to incorporate Buddhist philosophy. Prepare to notice the beauty of living things. Prepare to be at peace with yourself and who you are, and to take this journey knowing that it makes you feel less suffering and much more at peace with the world in which you live.

We have given you a lot of detail because it is a detailed philosophy and by splitting it into different sections covering what you need to know, you will easily be able to add parts of the philosophy to your life, wherever you may live and regardless of your lifestyle. Buddhism is for anyone who wishes to try it and is something that will enhance the way you view your life and everything that happens in it.

Chapter 4 – Steps 1 & 2 - Introduction of Buddhist Values into Your Life

Having generalized about what the Buddhist values are, you need to find a starting point so that you can see if they help your life and are suitable to incorporate into your lifestyle. That's the hard bit – knowing which values to add and whether you can keep to them. There are so many values that people who take on the ideas of Buddhism often try to incorporate too many at a time and get confused about it. It's better to introduce one at a time and get it right. Let's look at a step by step way of incorporating these into your life and give you a suggested order with examples of how you can make this work for you.

Step one - Introducing the Truth of Suffering

In this part of the introduction to Buddhist philosophy, you need to be aware that we all suffer and that the suffering that we have within our lives can be lessened. You need to admit that your life isn't perfect and be able to find forgiveness for past errors. We all make them and Buddhism admits that the suffering we have is as a consequence of our actions. Thus, the first place to begin this journey is to look at all the things that have happened in your life and forgive yourself for them. In the case of being wronged by others, you also have to accept that wrongs which are perceived as being directed toward you are only hurtful if you allowed them to be directed at you. Thus, forgiveness plays a huge part in peace of mind. Unless you can get past the bad stuff in your life, you will continue to suffer. What you need to write down are the things that trouble you about your life, in order to look at them and be able to let them go. There will be a variance in the kind of things that have happened.

- Some, within your control
- Some, which are outside of your control
- Some, which you believe to have been the fault of others

The Buddhist way of looking at these is very different from your standard way of looking at life. You can only be in control of your happiness if you are able to let go of things that do not contribute to. Thus, shame, blame and lack of forgiveness are all going to get in the way of your happiness. They have no point to them because they do not change what has happened. You can recognize what is wrong and what is right, but your own life need not be changed because of those values. What you can change is your level of understanding or forgiveness. Look at the list of things that make you unhappy. Which are within your control? These are the only things that you can change. For example, if you blame people or cannot forgive, you take the weight of the problem with you and it stops you from being at one with yourself. Thus, you need to try in this first step to look at things from a different perspective. If you have done wrong in the past, now is the time to forgive yourself. Only you can. If someone has wronged you, you cannot find peace in blame. Try to shake off that blame. Blame is a negative feeling and will resolve very little. If someone has done wrong, it is for them to put right. It is not your place in this life to take on unhappiness because of it.

I remember being startled at something that the Dalai Lama said about people praying for solutions to the recent shootings in Paris and although it was hard to swallow what he was saying, it was actually common sense. He said that we are praying to God to fix a problem caused by man himself. That is illogical and God would be within his rights to tell people to fix those problems themselves since they have caused them. Too often, we rely too heavily upon God for forgiveness and do not do the wise thing – which is to learn forgiveness ourselves. As long as we are aware that these things are wrong, then that's enough. There is little that the individual can do to make them happier than to show people around you that the loving and right way to be with others is always going to win. Thus, let go. Do not take anger with you because what anger does is fire up discontent and unhappiness and there is already too much of that in the world. By showing Buddhist philosophy within your life, you are able to let go of things that make you unhappy and of all the negative feelings that these things invoke.

I can give you a great example of letting go that really does help. After a violent argument on principle with someone dear to me, I was walking in a park and the anger was still churning in my mind. This was some years ago. I was letting that anger pound away at my head and it was making the situation much bigger than it actually was. Then I noticed something. A child in the playground area had his hand stuck at the top of the slide and was calling out for help. Of course, the natural thing for me to do was to run up the steps of the slide and help free the young child's hand. In that moment, I completely put my anger aside and it didn't matter to me during those moments of having a different priority. You need to see that holding onto blame when you can let go of it makes little sense. As long as you fill your moments with positive actions, then you replace all the negativity and that helps you to get to a state of happiness that is sustainable. That doesn't mean ignoring all the bad things around you. You can be aware of them, but you cannot let them change who you are fundamentally because when you do, the ugliness of the situation gets bigger. This demonstration was really to show how quickly a bad thought can be replaced with a good action and that's why Buddhists tend to live in the moment and why they also observe and learn without passing judgment. The moment that blame and judgment enter the picture, you lose that serenity because you introduce a negative element into your life.

Step two – Learning all about Karma

This is something that you learn about in Buddhism and Right Actions means that you must decide to take the right path toward others and toward all living creatures. You may argue that it seems a little strange when you think that Buddhists eat meat, but it isn't as strange as you may suppose. The Dalai Lama was trying to explain about the eating of meat and said that it is a strange quirk of Buddhism that in order to eat meat, animals need to be killed, so that suffering happens to produce that meat. However, the way that this is dealt with is that you must not harm the animals. It is understood that there will be people who work in the field of meat farming just as they may work in the field of crop farming. As long as you have not specifically ordered the killing of an animal or the animal has not been specifically killed to offer to you, then this is acceptable as a food. The Dalai Lama actually found this very difficult, since he had given up meat because he had seen a chicken slaughtered and it had upset him so much. However, health did not allow him to continue this regime and he had to go back to eating meat because his body had need of it, just as many others will have the same need for protein. Meat just happens to be part of the essential food chain.

Karma is what happens when you are cruel or when you do something that is not in following the right path toward others. If you purposely hurt someone, then it follows that you will be hurt. If you purposely kill something, then your justice will happen. You just don't know when this justice will take place. The Buddhists believe that when you perform something that is not right, you release energy into the world that in turn will come back to you. They also believe that there are states that man may be classified into according to their standing. These are as follows:

- **Bodhisattva** – This would be someone who would be destined to become the Buddha and who is there in order to teach others.

- **Pratyeka Buddha** – This would be the current Buddha

- **Sravka** – These would be people who follow the Buddha

- **Asura** – These are spirits who are fighting with life and trying to find their place

- **Preta** – These are bad people or people who Christians would consider would go to hell

If you are living a fairly moral life, then perhaps you would find yourself in the Sravka or Assura range, though what people do not realize is that their standing in life can change according to their actions and deeds and that's what Karma is all about. When you hear about someone coming back as a monkey, these are fables that have been invented in order to explain to people who do not understand karma, so that they are sufficiently motivated to try and be better than they currently are, by following Buddhist practice.

You cannot influence someone else's standing. Only they can do that. Thus, if there is evil within the world that you are judging, you need to step back and try to accept that each person performing evil will have a price to pay for that evil, just as each person trying harder to live in harmony with others may improve their status within the karmic system.

Your actions toward improving your Karma

What I would suggest is that you examine your attitude toward other living things and try to change it if you find that you are being either cruel or hurtful. Buddhist monks take this to extremes. In the movie, Seven Days in Tibet, we see the monks picking up worms when they were building the foundation for a theater. They did not want to harm the worms and were placing them in a jar to be removed to somewhere else that was safe. The way that you start to introduce better karma is to learn to be kind to yourself and to people around you. You also learn this from being kind to animals. Perhaps, in your case, this may just mean being more understanding toward a pet. It may mean feeling empathy for a friend or it may mean being consciously aware of not causing anyone suffering. Take a look at your life and you will see there are many ways that you can improve. These include:

- Cut down on excess meat

- Make sure that you are kind to animals

- Be kind to others

- Do not add to the suffering of others

These all improve your happiness status and also help you to become a better person so are good things to practice in your life. Being kind to someone who you would normally walk past in the street is being aware, not judging, but simply helping someone with a need. All of these positive actions in the moment are ones that will help you to raise your spiritual awareness so are positive actions for your improvement as a human being.

Chapter 5 – Step 3 – Introduction of Buddhist Values into Your Life

"Happiness is not something ready made. It comes from your own actions."

~ Dalai Lama

In this day and age people are teaching top executives something called Neuro Linguistic Programming and although not related to Buddhist practice, it is equally as beneficial if you understand why judgment of others is not something that is recommended in Buddhism. Neuro Linguistic Programming shows you how to look at things from different perspectives and gain a better understanding of the world, but it's very similar to the empathy that you show to people when you have Buddhist values. You do not judge. You observe and learn from that observation. That means that when things happen in your life, you are able to observe them and learn by putting yourself in the shoes of others. For example, if someone does you wrong, you do not see it as personal criticism, you see it as the failure of either communication or failure of that person to have sufficient understanding, but you don't act on it.

The way that we act with people who hurt us makes us more miserable than we need to be, when in fact empathy helps us to see why people do what they do. You see things from another perspective and are able to feel differently about the wrong. The only time that wrongdoing will affect who you are is if you let it. Let me try and give you an example. A man steals a loaf of bread, which means that you don't have bread to offer your family with their dinner. Instead of chastising the man, you would, under Buddhist laws, feel empathy for him and may even offer him another loaf, knowing that what you are doing is the right thing to do, considering that his circumstances are not as good as yours and besides which, your family are quite capable of finding another solution. This is one that westerners may find hard to appreciate, but what you are actually doing is showing someone peace and love and also teaching them a valuable lesson because they expect anger. When it is not shown, they feel humbled by your reaction and may think twice about the way that they approach things in the future.

Why did the man steal the bread? His need was more than yours and he had no money to buy any. Is it acceptable that he steals? Of course not, but his circumstances may have forced him into a situation where he had to make a choice. The point of all of this is that you need to learn empathy. Empathy is at the center of your understanding doing the right thing, or taking the right action. Taking the right action makes you stronger and when you start to incorporate giving and understanding, empathy and being able to see different viewpoints into your life, it enriches it, and you become more generous and capable of being a better person.

Unfortunately, in the west, we live in a world where judgments are given all of the time without any form of empathy. If someone doesn't measure up to our standards, we criticize them. If they don't dress the way others do, we judge them. If they choose to live a life that is outside the scope of our own lives, we tend to be opinionated about how wrong that choice is.

The Buddhist way is to observe, but not to pass judgment, so this is something that you can add to your second week of trying to use Buddhist philosophy. When you are able to drop judgment and to see things as they really are, you open up your eyes to new possibilities but you also become happier because your life is no longer ruled by what society believes is right. It is ruled by what you are willing to accept and in accepting that people don't all fit the mold perfectly, you become more tolerant and understanding.

Remember always:

Right understanding, Right attitude, Right speech, Right Action

These form a part of the Buddhist philosophy. Right understanding means having a balanced view of the things that happen within your life. Looking at them in a non- judgmental way and being able to use these for lessons in your life. When you use right understanding – you don't tend to get angry and annoyed at people. You simply observe actions and understand that there are reasons why things happen. Right attitude means the attitude with which you receive events that happen in your life. Instead of getting angry or taking those misfortunate incidents in your life to another level of negativity, you examine them – you use empathy to understand them and you are able to remain happy. Right speech means saying the right things and those should be well thought out messages that are never intended to hurt or wound and right action means putting the whole package together and being able to learn from it and move into the next moment with no regrets, because it is only when this attitude, speech, understanding and action lead to negative scenarios that you learn nothing.

Thus, these are things that you can incorporate into your life and start to see that life is much more balanced than you perhaps perceived it to be. It will help you to start to feel an inner peace that perhaps you have had missing from your life and that's when you really do know that you are doing something right.

Chapter 6 – Abstaining from Alcohol and Drugs

"Where ignorance is our master, there is no possibility of real peace."

~ Dalai Lama

Although you may not have thought of this aspect of Buddhism, right action will include disallowing you to do certain things. This means that the following actions are not permitted if you want to keep the Buddhist philosophy in your life:

- Over indulgence in alcohol or stimulants
- Stealing
- Misuse of sex
- Killing
- Lying

You may wonder what the Dalai Lama says about drugs, bearing in mind that medical marijuana has been something that has hit the news recently, in that it is generally accepted that it can help people with pain. Putting medical use to one side, which the Dalai Lama says is between doctor and patient, he believes that the use of alcohol and drugs is very bad because it distorts what you see and can actually damage your perception which is something that Buddhists would find hard to live with.

The Elephant Journal was quoted as saying "The basic Buddhist teachings on alcohol consumption are quite clear. Alcohol, the Buddha taught more than 2,000 years ago, is a poison that clouds the inherent clarity of the mind." It went on to say that not all Buddhist centers are like this but that when alcohol is introduced to a social event, there has to be mindfulness while you are drinking it for a specific purpose. As a means to relax, a few sips of beer or wine are acceptable, though if you go further than the relaxation stages, then you are in danger of excess. Traditional Buddhist centers will not serve alcohol and these are likely to be zones that do not offer that alternative, though in Vajrayana practices this is more acceptable.

To help you to get this into perspective, no one is going to get up tight if you have a few sips to help you to get into a relaxed state of mind, but excess is definitely not where it's at. When you are drinking, you take small sips. You savor the taste and allow your mind to enjoy what little you have. Excess is not a Buddhist thing. This small amount of alcohol is all that your mind requires and any more than that can actually damage the way that you approach your Buddhism practice because it can distort life and damage the concepts that you had previously established. For example, someone who is drunk is not likely to take Right action and since this is a fundamental rule in Buddhism, drunkenness should be avoided.

In many treatment centers, Buddhist practice is used to help people who have addictions conquer them. People who take up meditation are taught how to recognize triggers of their addictions and are also taught what freedom of personal development these stimulants may actually deprive someone of. In meditation practice, one needs to be totally mindful and if you deprive yourself of the mindfulness by using too much alcohol or too many drugs, you also deprive yourself of the potential joy that can you can achieve from the activity of meditation.

Several tips have been given by Buddhist monks on the subject of alcohol and drugs and the most astute ask you to recognize the triggers and instead of allowing yourself the stimulant, concentrating on the freedom that you get if you resist that stimulant or that you deprive yourself of if you succumb. Often people can use their craving to redirect their energies. It's a strong craving, but instead of satisfying it by giving into it, you can use this as a catalyst to becoming a better and more conscious person. This energy may be exactly what you need in order to meditate.

When the Dalai Lama was asked about whether he had indulged in alcohol, he laughed and told the story about when he was a young boy and was given a bottle of wine. His only taste of it was on the end of his finger, though he had never indulged in drinking alcohol in his life. Thus, for this part of your challenge to move toward a Buddhist philosophy, try to limit the amount of alcohol you drink and use cravings as a sign that you need to meditate. The keywords of a Buddhist lifestyle is to "Do no harm" and that means to yourself as well as to others. Stealing and lying and misusing sexuality can also be harmful to others, so should be avoided if you want to follow the right path. The excesses of life are generally the things that are frowned upon and that can include eating to excess or indulging in anything excessively that may be harmful to you. Thus, think in moderation and you will be on the right track.

Alcohol and drugs are thought of as distorting what you see and this would be something that would be very hard to incorporate into a Buddhist way of thinking since the clarity of the mind is so important to Buddhists. Thus, limit your intake and learn to use your mind in better ways and you will be heading in the right direction.

Chapter 7 – Being Kind and Spreading Happiness

"Compassion is all inclusive. Compassion knows no boundaries. Compassion comes with awareness, and awareness breaks all narrow territories."

~ Amit Ray

One of the easiest ways to incorporate Buddhism into your life is in your attitude toward others. Compassion forms part of that but so does empathy. Empathy isn't just feeling good thoughts toward people. It means actually being able to put yourself in their shoes. That takes quite a bit of doing, but when you learn to do it, you will find yourself much more compassionate. The Dalai Lama says that it's a Buddhist's lot to share happiness and to spread it and that doesn't take a lot of changes in your life. It means changing things step by step.

Start to smile more – Smiling is thought of by Buddhists as being open with people and you will always find in western society that smiles actually encourage smiles. That's why people love to watch things that make them laugh or that spread joy. There is so much bad stuff in our lives today that spreading happiness is something that adds something very positive to someone else's day as well as to your own.

You may not know it, but every time that you spread joy you are adding positivity to your life. For example, instead of passing the beggar on the street and ignoring his need, how about passing him a sandwich if you are suspicious about parting with money? It is small gestures toward mankind that are huge leaps in the right direction as far as Buddhism is concerned. The Dalai Lama always tells us that the principle mission of the Buddhist is to spread positivity and hope and that's not a bad message to send to people that pass through your life.

If you take the time to read the words of the Dalai Lama on his webpage, the message that he is giving everyone is all about the intention of man and the purpose of his life. That is to seek happiness. No one wants to be miserable. No one wants to be seen as the bad sport, the selfish egoist or the person who makes others unhappy, but little do people realize the impact that happiness has on self and how all of the acts that you do in your life translate as far as mentality goes. It's a bit of an understatement when he says, "From my own limited experience, I have found that the greatest degree of tranquility comes from the development of love and compassion" and he is of course very right. When you are able to incorporate love and compassion into your life, you begin to be able to find inner happiness, such that you would never find had you carried on with selfish ways.

The other thing that you find when you spread happiness is that you feel an inner peace. For example, I have given some cases below which may be experiences that you have every day of the week in which you can actually incorporate Buddhist philosophy to try and make things better than they are:

Person that works with you is unhappy – Take time to listen without judgment. That's one Buddhist principle that isn't as easy as it sounds. While many of us criticize people because they are so negative, instead of doing that – listen and empathize. Realize what it's like being on the other side of the fence and try to see things from the perspective of the other person.

Wife, Husband or Children are complaining – Although these may be the kind of things that you take in your stride, go one step further than usual. Learn empathy and make all the right responses. That doesn't mean giving in to bad ideas. That means learning what the root problem is and helping them to solve it. Stop looking at the world as a place where everyone is out to get what they can and start seeing the bigger picture. If people are expressing any kind of unhappiness, you can help them to solve those problems and become happier. Logic and listening come into play and if you can make people who mean a lot to you see sense in a situation such as this and come out of the situation with a positive outlook, you will have achieved your aim.

Help someone who deserves it - The Buddhist people are very giving. They feel that if someone has something and someone else doesn't, there is a kind of imbalance and they are right to a certain degree. Give your neighbor something nice. If you have an old person in the neighborhood, why not buy them or make them something that they will really appreciate. A hot casserole may be very welcomed by a senior that lives on their own, but more than that, stopping by and listening adds something to their day that would not otherwise have happened. Remember, our old folk were young once and were able to get out and about. Perhaps you can help them by doing the shopping for them or running some chores. It isn't just children who do this for pocket money. People do it too for no reward whatsoever. When you are giving, give with absolutely no expectation of anything in return. It makes the giving much purer and is how Buddhist philosophy expects giving to be. That's a good practice for you to try. If you want to help someone by giving, do so with no strings attached and do so for the benefit of someone that needs it because that's following

Buddhist philosophy. If you have something that someone else needs and they have more use of it than you, then you would be justified in giving because you are enhancing someone else's life and making it a more positive thing.

Chapter 8 – Being Mindful

"The roots of all goodness lie in the soil of appreciation for goodness."

~ Dalai Lama

We have introduced another section on mindfulness but this chapter is all about what you can do, step by step during your day to be mindful. It's all about noticing the world around you and appreciating what you see. People who do not appreciate their world are those who are usually too busy within that world to notice the things that count. Perhaps you have even found yourself in their number, because the world is indeed a very fast place. The first thing that you need to do here is to learn the breathing techniques that help you. The reason for this is to make you more aware of your own inner strengths and weaknesses. You do need to be aware of your body and of your thought processes to use meditation, but the exercises within this chapter are ones that help you move toward being mindful.

You are probably not accustomed to relaxation in the true sense of the word. Perhaps your idea of relaxation is sitting in front of the TV and watching a favorite movie, and that's okay, but it may not include mindfulness. To make the most of every moment of your life, under Buddhist philosophy, you need to be aware of your breathing, your posture and every sense that is part of the moment that you are in.

Exercise in breathing

For this exercise, sit in a comfortable position on a hard chair and make sure that your back is completely straight. This alignment is very important because it allows the energy to flow through your chakras that are your energy points. These are located all over the body. If you can think of the air that you breathe as a force of energy that is something that you can see, this helps you to understand how the exercises help you. You don't just breathe in the way that you normally breathe. Normally you breathe and don't give much thought to it. It's an automatic process that you have always grown up with and perhaps you find it strange that you are exercising your breathing or learning a new way. The purpose of this is so that you feel the flow of energy and can latch onto it as something very positive, happening within your body that allows you to gain energy.

Close your eyes because too much distraction may take you away from the meaning of the process. Breathe in deeply through the nose to the count of five, and then hold that breathe inside you to the count of six. As you are breathing in, feel the upper diaphragm grow and then breathe out, counting to seven. Do this over and over until you find that you are doing this naturally. The problem that people get these days is that they tend to over-oxygenate their bodies and this is what leads to stress. Too much oxygen in the system and everything works too quickly. The idea of breathing exercises is to teach you to tell your body to slow down and do things at a pace that is beneficial. Do this over and over again. It really will give you energy.

Second breathing exercise

This is an exercise that is useful for you if you find that you are always tired at the end of the day and need more energy to get you through the day. It can be practiced alone and in privacy, but what it does is wake up part of you that may otherwise be dormant. It's a wonderful exercise that helps you to take advantage of the energy of your breathing if you need to gain extra strength during a busy time in your life. Take a seated position and make sure that you are comfortable and have no distractions. This is important because a tight waistband, for example, can make you feel very uncomfortable, and you need to put all your concentration on your breathing techniques. These are used by Buddhist monks and are useful to help you to gain spiritual energy.

Hold the thumb of your left hand over your right nostril and breathe in. Hold the breath and while you are holding it, move the thumb to your other nostril and then breathe out. Do this over again, this time using the second nostril first. You need to do this about a dozen times for it to have effect, but while you are doing this be conscious only of your breathing and nothing else that is happening around you. It is this awareness of the breathing and awareness of self that is important to the technique.

Why you do alternate nostril breathing

Your right and left nostrils have different senses. The left nostril is used for calming down your mind while the other is used to gain energy. Thus, when you alternately use the nostrils for your breathing, what you are doing is working on that part of your brain that you may otherwise neglect and you become more mindful of the benefits of the breathing to you. This kind of breathing has many benefits. It is known to make the mind sharper, to relax the body and to clear out the lungs of impurities. The best time to practice it for the benefits to the lungs are first thing in the morning and when you come in after a day's work. Five minutes of breathing in this way will help your relaxation levels and will also help you to get rid of all the impurities that may be lurking in the bottom of your lungs.

Whenever you do breathing exercises, be completely mindful of the process that you are going through. In other words be aware of it. These breathing techniques help you to become more aware and will make you a much more relaxed person. You are oxygenating your system in a very healthy way and are, at the same time, stimulating your nervous system that means that you are more in touch with your body and mind and Buddhism is wrapped around the premise that you should become more enlightened in your life. That includes knowing your body and the everyday functions of it a little better and since all of this starts with breathing, what better place to begin?

Appreciating the environment in which you find yourself

This is another aspect of mindful behavior. Wherever you are, notice it and take it in because it may be the last time that you see what you are able to see. The flowers in the park or the cobwebs on the trees, think of each moment as precious. Being mindful isn't just about living. It's about knowing you are living and taking in every experience that you have with the same amount of enthusiasm and awareness. It's about being aware of people less well off than you and trying to help. It's about letting go of selfishness and greed and all of the other negative aspects of life because none of these will make you happy and that's the ultimate goal of Buddhism. Be aware, taste the fruits of life and enjoy every moment that you have.

If you can incorporate meditation, this will help you as well and in the next chapter, we have that covered. Meditation is not some religious act. It's the act of replenishing and this is really important to the Buddhist religion. Getting to know your inner mind and making peace between your mind and body are all part and parcel of the philosophy and you can incorporate that into your life quite easily. Yes, it's a struggle at first, but you do become accustomed to it and that's something you need to persevere with. When Buddhists meditate, they do so because they want to reach that Nirvana which is a deeper understanding. You cannot get there by external forces, but need to use inwardly looking to balance up the chakras and to also balance the harmony between mind and body.

Chapter 9 – Practicing Meditation

"Calm mind brings inner strength and self-confidence, so that's very important for good health."

~ Dalai Lama

This forms a part of the Buddhist culture. When Siddhartha went out into the desert to try and find answers to the question of why humanity suffers so much, he used meditation to come up with the answers. Historically speaking, what he found through his meditation was the answer to all unhappiness and suffering caused to and by mankind. It was this revelation that spurred him onto writing out how people could get away from suffering. His enlightenment was what people aim for when they meditate. The clarity with which you begin to see problems is amazing, though it does take time for you to get to that stage, so you need to be very patient indeed.

In your home, you need to create a space where you can go that is peaceful and tranquil and where you will not be disturbed. There is no need to have a Buddha statue, but if this makes you feel happy, then of course you can add things such as this to the room and dedicate it to your meditation. However, there is no obligation. Meditation is something that anyone can do in a peaceful spot and with minimal props and inspirational material. The part that you will find particularly difficult is being able to think of nothing. That's why systems were invented whereby you don't have to think of nothing but are given specific things to concentrate on instead. There are two types of meditation used by Buddhists and one may suit you better than another.

One of these is the use of the Om or the chant. During meditation, you repeat the chant and you concentrate solely on the production of the sound and the sound itself. This is helpful for people who are not very good at concentrating on nothing. Test yourself. Sit in a darkened room and close your eyes and see how long you can last without actually thinking about things. It won't be very long at all because our minds are not trained to work like that. From childhood, you start to think of a series of words and then learn their meaning and these words go together and form chains of thoughts. Thus, the mind is always active. When you meditate, you are not shutting it down, but you are concentrating all of your effective thought on a specific thing. This can be breathing or it can be a chant and the choice is yours.

Chanting

The reason that you use a word that means very little to you is simple. You cannot then expect the mind to go onto the chain of thought because the word is meaningless. The Om sound is produced with the lips, though if you have a Tibetan singing bowl, this can set the scene giving you a pitch that you may like to work to. Your lips should be slightly apart and when you chant the word Om, you should feel a slight vibration on your lips. If you don't, adjust your lips a little until you do. This sound is something that you need to make from your upper abdomen right the way out of your mouth and concentrate on it totally.

Concentrating on breathing

If you choose to opt for this method of meditation, your breathing needs to be practiced and you need to remember that your back should always be straight when you are meditating. This helps the flow of energy through your chakras and that's vital for good health. You breathe in through the nose to the count of five, hold the breath for the count of six and breathe out either through the nose or mouth to the count of seven. While you are doing this, you need to be totally conscious of the energy or air going into your body, of staying within your body and then of leaving it. During this time, you think of nothing other than that energy.

At the end of each exhale, you count one to ten and then start back at one again. There is another way of doing this if you don't want to concentrate on numbers and that's to use meditation beads because as you work your way around the meditation beads and get to the beginning of the beads, you will know that your session is over. Whether you work twice around the beads of more depends upon you. It's your choice but it means that you have some means of measuring the time that you spend meditating and can break off from meditation when you feel that you have done enough for the day.

How often to meditate

If you really want to incorporate Buddhist ways into your lifestyle, then once a day at a minimum should be spent on meditation but at the beginning when you are new to it, fifteen minutes per session is enough. You can increase that when you get better at meditation.

Why do people meditate?

Buddhists meditate in order to try and work their way to Nirvana, which is that place of understanding and enlightenment. Other people may meditate because they find that it brings out the spiritual side of their nature and yet others will meditate because they find it beneficial from a health point of view. During meditation, your blood pressure will go down and the changes that happen within your body are very beneficial indeed. Your heart rate will slow, your metabolism will change and you will get to feel very relaxed which is good for all kinds of illnesses. Meditation also helps you in your concentration levels and if you have a lot of problems, it can help you to find the inner strength to get through bad stages in your life and to find answers. After you meditate, you go quietly back into the world and you will find that you have a sharper sense of awareness, that you are more alert and that you are able to do a lot more than you could before you meditated. Thus, it can help you to become much more productive.

Meditation

You need to find a position that is comfortable. Some people like the full lotus position where your feet are tucked in but if you are new to the practice of meditation, it's unlikely that you are supple enough to do this. Don't worry. There are no set rules about your position, except that your back should be straight. Newcomers are best sitting on a cushion on the floor, bending their legs and crossing their ankles. It's a lot easier for beginners. Also, make sure that you have comfortable clothing on. The full process of meditation is explained in another chapter. However, this chapter is really about preparing yourself and practicing the silence in your mind. Sit and breathe as you have been shown and think only of the breath going in and out of your body. Otherwise, think only of the chant of the Om sound.

You may also want to try walking meditation that is helpful to people who merely want a break from their day. In walking meditation you look downward so that you don't trip but you concentrate on your breathing in the same way and take strides as you think. I tend to do this kind of meditation when I am busy at work and need a break to think things through and it's an easy kind of meditation to fit into your day. The paces that you take, the breaths that you take and the concentration on these things means that you are giving your mind a much needed rest from thinking about negative things.

Chapter 10 - Introducing Mindfulness in Detail

"Human happiness and Human satisfaction must ultimately come from within oneself"

~ Dalai Lama

It is not enough to feel mindful. You also need to act in a way that shows care for others. Without action, belief and mindfulness are pretty meaningless, but in this chapter we look at what mindfulness is all about because this will help you to see how you can begin to improve your lot in life. Place one of your favorite chocolates into your mouth. Close your eyes and taste that chocolate. Feel it melt upon your tongue and enjoy every single suck. Mindfulness is concentrating on the moment and letting everything else slip into insignificance. It's not a trade in. It's actually learning to live in the moment and to take from that moment in your life everything that it has to offer.

Mindfulness also makes you aware of others. You can use it to help someone else. It isn't all about you. For instance, if you are walking in the park and see someone drop a bag of groceries, it doesn't hurt to drop everything you are doing and go to help them. Mindfulness makes you aware of others but not judgmental. When Buddhist monks meditate, many of them have their eyes open to the world. When you first learn meditation, you need your eyes closed because you are not yet accustomed to being able to discipline your mind. As you get more disciplined and are able to meditate with your eyes open, you start to see that the things around you should not change the way that you think. You should not derive negative thoughts from them.

People who are not at peace with their lives tend to let their minds wander back to moments that have passed and are filled with remorse and regret. Those with self-esteem issues dwell on things that people have said to them and feel worse about themselves because they let these thoughts and actions penetrate and become more important than the actual reality. If you call someone names for long enough, that person is programmed to think that they merit those names. However, no one really is. Meditation helps you to switch off the voices of the past or the worries of the future and just be present in that moment in time and that's valuable because it's a better place to be than to be constantly upset over things that people have said, and it's certainly healthier than thinking about tomorrow, which hasn't come yet. Mindfulness is always in the now.

Exercises to achieve mindfulness

We want you to achieve mindfulness. The reason it is so important is because it makes the moment count for something. There are several exercises included in this chapter so that you can indeed enjoy this moment in your life and be completely present within that moment. Remember what the Dalai Lama said about people being too busy or too obsessed with the material side of life to actually enjoy the moment that they are in. What we need to show you is how to incorporate mindfulness into a moment of your day, and then to use this exercise in the moments that follow. You won't achieve it completely at first, as you are programmed to think about things that are other than in this moment in time, but when you get good at this, what you do is take away the pressures of life and make life much more rewarding for yourself. You find a sense of peace, a sense of acceptance and a sense of being in that moment, instead of wasting it by throwing that moment away with thoughts of the past or future.

For this exercise, go into the garden or into a park and sit somewhere where you can see the wonders of nature in front of you. Observe them. Try to retain as much information on what you see as you can. The tree colors – the sky color – the color of blossoms – the color of the grass. When you think that you have absorbed everything, close your eyes and still see it. Recount everything that you saw and open your eyes and see how accurate you were.

The next exercise is one in hope. When you light a candle, the flame is symbolic. It can symbolize all kinds of things. You may light it for a person who has died, to bring their soul into this moment in time. You may light it to warm your heart and make you feel happy. You may even light it to enjoy the diminished light rather than electrical light. To get the best of this exercise, choose your location. For example, if you want perfumed candles around a bathtub, that's okay. If you want to light a candle in a darkened room, that works and if you want to enter a church a light a candle, then that's fine too. It's what you want to get out of it that matters. Light the candle. Think of nothing except the flame of the candle. Lose yourself in it and think of nothing else.

What you gain from these exercises is something that you can dwell on in that moment in time. This focuses you in that particular moment. From eating, through to walking in the rain, being present in the moment helps you to shed all the sadness from the past, to stop being judgmental and to start seeing life in true perspective. This moment may be the only one you have and when you learn not to waste those moments, you begin to see life from a new perspective.

You need to allow your mind to separate itself from the past and to stop worrying about the future since these moments in time are not now. Now is the important thing to remember and to live in and by being able to do that you will achieve much. You will drop anger and resentment and all the negativity that may go hand in hand with past events. They are not now. They do not define who you are unless you let them define it. You need to enjoy the moment that you are in because this is much more relevant. The following poem sums it up because it shows you what can happen in a moment in time:

Hold out your hand and touch the summer sun,

Watch shadows chase through trees to forest floor,

Enjoy the moment and until it's past and done,

Do not spend time in wishing it was more.

Because in every moment that you pass,

There is a richness that you can behold,

The dewdrops dancing on a blade of grass,

The leaves that fall in autumn turned to gold.

In mindful meditation you can find your soul,

Will see all that it needs to see to find its focus,

Each fragment in that moment is quite whole,

Without the need for dreams and hocus pocus,

All that you need is just to stop and take it in,

Embracing that which senses feel or eat,

Forgetting past regrets and other's sin,

To make yourself feel happy and complete.

Elizabeth Ward

Chapter 11 – Introducing Peace

"Human happiness and human satisfaction must ultimately come from inside oneself"

~ Dalai Lama

The overall purpose of Buddhism's Truths is so that you understand the cause of suffering and can find a way in your life to avoid that suffering. Peace comes from understanding that only you control how you feel. Depression and many forms of human suffering come from judging situations in a negative manner. For example, your father in law says to you "I don't like the way you dress" and people who make this their problem see the comment as negatively affecting the way that they interact with their father in law. However, this can be approached in another way. Understanding is what it's all about. Instead of the silence that follows a negative comment such as this, why not explore it. "What is it that you don't like?" is not insulting. It's inquiring. There can be all kinds of reasons why people see negatives and once you learn compassion and empathy, you can see things so much more clearly. "It reminds me too much of my late wife," may have been his answer. You see it's not all about you. It never is. When comments are made to you, try and see from another perspective some positive message that comes from what you hear. Do not always assume blame.

You find peace when you accept who you are and what you are and are happy within yourself. Do no harm to others. Learn to be who you are and be true to that person you believe yourself to be. There is never the need for arguing which always leaves someone feeling negative. Look into your heart for answers and if you can't find them try empathy.

Meditation is part of finding that peace within yourself. To meditate, you must find a position that is comfortable. People meditate in the lotus position, but that's too hard for beginners. Try propping up your behind on a cushion and bending your legs at the knees. Then cross the ankles. The most important thing is that your back is straight as this allows energy to pass through your body easily. Your head should be straight and your middle finger should touch your thumb so that you don't fiddle around nervously with your hands. Place these onto your knees.

Buddhist meditation takes on a very simple method. You breathe, but you don't think of breath as simple breathing. Think of it as energy. Breathe in through the nose and concentrate on the energy going into your body as you do so. Hold the breath for a moment and then breathe out through the nose. Your mind should concentrate solely on breathing because meditation is about letting go of thoughts. When the original Buddha reached Nirvana, he didn't do so by giving up. He did so by perseverance and that's what Buddhist monks seek. In your case, you are seeking a peaceful place where you subconscious can rest. Close your eyes. Breathe in that energy, hold it for a moment and then breathe out, thinking of nothing but the breathing or energy. Then count to one. Do the same and count to two and so on until you reach ten. If you find thoughts entering your mind, start back at one. You may not know it, but your subconscious works very hard if you let it. Often your mind is so filled up with thoughts that the subconscious cannot make sense of anything. During meditation, however, it's energizing and working away in the background, so that you are unaware of its working, but will still feel the benefit of that work that it is doing. You will feel refreshed and ready to tackle the world again after meditation, but should rise slowly and relax your way back into your daily routine.

The inner peace that you feel when you meditate is because you are putting away all the worldly troubles that may have been filling your mind and allowing your mind the rest that it needs. All your negative thoughts are put neatly away in little boxes, allowing your mind to flow in a much more peaceful way. When you do that, you learn a little about the peace that the original Buddha found took him away from suffering. Buddhists do not believe in suffering. Nor do they believe in inflicting harm on any living soul. When you can embrace their thoughts and include knowing that you should never harm yourself, you begin to see how your thought processes work and are more conscious of actions that actually do you harm. For example, if you don't like yourself very much, you need to learn to love yourself, regardless of what other people say.

I knew someone once who was left by the person she loved. She dwelled on that parting for many months. Unfortunately, she saw her life as over because the person she loved didn't love her any more. When I first talked about self-love to her, she couldn't understand that concept at all. She felt that she needed a man and she felt that no one would possibly love her again, but what she had failed to see was the longer she hated who she was, the further she placed herself from ever loving herself.

Self-love includes many different things. It doesn't mean that you need to be completely happy with everything you are as you will change and evolve. It means that you are happy with what you give back to the world and that nothing will stop you from being able to do that. You are happy within yourself because you are doing the best that you can. When she eventually started on that track, she actually found that she was attracting more friendships and genuine ones at that, because she was in herself a much more accepting and powerful friend to have.

We get so wrapped up in troubles that sometimes we don't see beyond them. If you imagine the man that fears the dark. He will be afraid of the night and will not see that the day quickly follows the night and will give him the light that makes him feel happier. When you are in a situation that makes you negative, you don't see beyond the negativity. Another man who hates the night understands that sleep is the best way to get through it and will sleep those hours away and be perfectly happy. The Dalai Lama says that if you wake every day and you want to be happy, treat everyone you meet with kindness and he is right. Kindness goes a long way toward making you happy and the people around you happy. Thus, when you look at fear, treat yourself kindly as well and you will be able to get through nights even though you have fear.

It's how you accept life and what it offers you that determines how happy you are within yourself and the Buddhist philosophy reinforces the idea that everyone has the capability of finding happiness by keeping to the general rules which are laid down for monks, although you don't have to be a monk to incorporate many of them into your life. Look at what these rules are and they are common sense things that happy people already do. Being conscious of them, you are more likely to be able to incorporate them and become happy as a result.

Right View – See things in a more positive way

Right Intentions – Always be honest in your actions and have the right motives

Right Speech – Learn to say things that offer kindness and leave negativity behind

Right Action – Do the right thing

Right Livelihood – Take up work that harms no one

Right Effort – Always do your best

Right Concentration – Put everything you are into what you do. Do nothing half-heartedly.

Right Mindfulness – Be mindful at all times

These are the eight fold paths of Buddhism and although you may not be able to keep to all of them, the more you can keep to, the happier you are likely to be. There's a very good reason for that. Each of these is geared toward positivity toward yourself and toward others and positivity feeds happiness.

When you put all of these or as many as you can into your life, you find a new kind of peacefulness. This includes the kind of behavior you have toward yourself so if you suffer from self-esteem problems, you need to start looking at yourself more kindly and seeing all the good things that you are capable of, rather than looking at the bad things. This is the Right View.

You may need to read through this chapter again and try to concentrate on using the exercises of seeing things in the right way before you get the hang of it. It's not that hard once you have achieved it. Think of your current situation and think of how you can incorporate all the right things into your life to make it a richer place to be. Let's reiterate these values and see them as they may appear to you in this moment in time:

Right View – Notice the weather and the wonders of nature around you

Right Intentions – Do something nice for someone else right now. It only takes small gestures. Make your partner a coffee.

Right Speech – Telephone a friend and be positive and uplifting. It helps their day and it will also help yours.

Right Action – Take a positive action. Maybe you can offer to help someone or say a kind word to a child.

Right Livelihood – Enjoy the chores that you have to do around the house and do them with humility seeing each of these with equal importance.

Right Effort – Do everything that you do in the best way that you can. This even includes sweeping the floor. Make the job as good as you can make it.

Right Concentration – Put everything you are into what you do. Do nothing half-heartedly. We said this before, but are reinstating it because that's the way you look at the things you have to do in your life.

Chapter 12 – Observation

"As long as we live in a human society, we have to depend upon each other. No one can survive as an island."

~ Dalai Lama

Sometimes, we cut ourselves off from people because it's easier than facing life. However, as the Dalai Lama says, we cannot be islands. We live in a human society and one of the best ways of learning happiness is to simply observe. Observation allows us to see bad behavior, good behavior, beauty, depth and every attribute a human being may display and it helps us to draw lines in our lives as to what is acceptable and what is not as far as our own actions are concerned. The problem comes when you observe things from a critical point of view because this isn't the Buddhist way. In the last chapter, we talked about the **Right View** and that means seeing the world as a Buddhist would. It is not for us to make judgments, but to learn from what we see what we need to encompass within our own lives.

Try an exercise in observation because it does the soul good and it teaches you that somehow you aren't in the worst situation in the world, even though at times it may feel as though you are. The world in which we live is vast. Observation helps you to get things into perspective and also makes you more empathetic. There are those who mistake this word as being "sympathetic" but it's a totally different thing. When you see a beggar on the street, can you put yourself in his shoes? That's what empathy allows you to do.

Try sitting in a public place and observing without judgment. It's not that easy, but after a while of doing this, you begin to see that people are struggling with life just as much as you are and that if you add any negativity to the situation, you don't make it better. In fact, you can make yourself and others even unhappier. Let's try and demonstrate this, by taking a seat in a local café and telling you what I am observing, as it is happening. There are several ways of looking at the world and if you don't have the **Right View**, then you add to your own misery or to the misery of others.

There's a girl over the table from me who has a young child. She has very little control over the child and is struggling with it. There are two ways of looking at this. One could be critical and say that girls like her shouldn't have kids, or you can be empathetic and understand that the girl is struggling and if you can lend a hand, you may make the situation easier. If you have the experience to do that, then giving one moment of your time can make the world of difference to her and to you.

Do not assume yourself to be better than her or stand in judgment because that isn't the right way to view her and her circumstances. Instead, place yourself in her shoes and see how difficult life is. The girl may have made a mistake in her life and is paying for that mistake. She doesn't need the judgment of others to make it even worse. I was once in a doctor's surgery when there was a young girl with a child waiting as well. The child was bored. There was not much to do in the surgery waiting room and the child was getting difficult for the girl to handle. I handed over my iPad to the kiddy and he instantly had something to occupy his mind with a game of Angry Birds. Sometimes, you just need to read situations without judgment and help out where you can.

Back to the café – there's a girl struggling to stay upright in high heeled shoes. She looks like she has no confidence at all. Society these days encourages people to mock others, but the Buddhist way of looking at things the Right Way would be to feel empathy. The poor girl is trying to look good. She obviously thinks that she is too short and is trying to elevate herself. Feel empathy. Feel understanding because in this day and age, we tend to see standards in magazines and if we don't conform to those standards, have self-esteem issues. When you see things from a different viewpoint and can look without judgment, you learn a lot about human nature. You learn to observe and not to use negative interaction or make fun of people because of their circumstances. The girl at the back of the café is struggling with weight. Do you think it helps her happiness levels to be called "fat?" Of course it doesn't, but empathy allows you to see people in unfortunate situations and be more understanding.

The right view will always prompt you to help when you can. It won't prompt you to proffer opinion because your opinion is no more valuable than anyone else's and the moment that you think it is, you fail. You may know how to do something and be able to help someone else to learn how to do it out of kindness. That's the right view. However, never impose yourself on others when your help is unwarranted and unwanted. The purpose of observation is to teach yourself inner peace with the world. It's a way to teach yourself the right view:

A man is struggling down the street. He is homeless. He has no winter clothes and it's pretty cold. He looks hungry.

The right view: Can I help this man? Can I buy him a coffee or a sandwich? Do I have clothing at home that would be useful to this man?

The wrong view: He is homeless and should find work and provide for himself.

You don't know the circumstances. You don't know what goes on inside his heart and mind and things are not nearly as simplistic as our minds may at first tell us. The right view and the one that makes you a happier person is the one that doesn't judge but that interacts in a very positive way with people along the road of your life that you are able to help. The Buddhist way doesn't mock, doesn't judge, doesn't assume. It merely observes and helps wherever it can.

Interactions that you have with others will give you negative or positive thoughts. The reason that you are seeking some new way is that you are pretty unhappy with the way in which your life is going. Thus, the sacrifice that you must make in order to become happy is to stop being judgmental and start to see each moment in your life as it unfolds and accept it for what it is. You cannot change the fact that there are millions of homeless in the world. You cannot change that there is injustice. You cannot do very much about the wars that are going on all over the world.

However, you can give help where you are able and if more people take this view, there will be less people suffering. There's a system that's rather good that I found whereby I could loan someone $25 through a website for a good purpose. I can't imagine living in a place that cannot drink the water because it will make people ill. However, the $25 that I have loaned will pay for a filter so that a family within that situation can have safe water. They, in turn, will supply villagers with safe water and eventually, as time allows, pay me back. I was surprised about the 90 percent return rate that these people in dire circumstances pay back those loans. They don't wish to be in debt. They simply want to improve their lot in life and $25 really isn't a lot to give whether I ever see it again or not. The point that I am making is that where you are able to change the world starts within your head by seeing things in the right way.

It is easy to switch channels on the TV when things happen on the news that we don't want to face up to. Our lives are complex enough as it is. However, when you take the route of the Buddhist philosophy, you see things in a different light. You feel compassion. You feel moved to positive action, even if that action is humble in comparison with needs. You don't judge. You simply observe and interact with people as and when you can and it makes you feel a lot happier inside.

Exercise in Humility

Bake a cake. Bake it because you want the cake to be a good one. Pack it into a box and give it to a neighbor. You are not seeking thanks. You are seeking nothing but giving. You are not seeking praise or gratitude. You don't know your neighbor's situation, but you do know that she is old and lives alone. Do it for her and expect nothing. Gifts that have no strings attached are the most liberating gifts. They bind people together and they make friendships.

The Right Action at the right time really can help uplift both you and her and that's when you start to see yourself as passing a moment of positivity. Observe her smile and be happy that it was you who caused it. Don't expect it. When you go to give a gift to a stranger, expect nothing. The point is that we don't know other people's unhappiness. We don't know what causes them to be sad or miserable.

Perhaps the next door neighbor keeps herself tucked away because she cannot escape her own unhappiness. Perhaps she has bad experiences of life. Even if the neighbor slams the door in your face, be happy that you gave because you don't know why that happened and it's not your place to judge. Your job was to bake a cake and give it and be happy that you have given it. Anything more than that takes you into the realms of expectation and it's when you expect others to act in a set way that you experience disappointment.

Parents sometimes remind children "I have made sacrifices for you." By doing so, they lay guilt upon the doorsteps of their children. The choice of making sacrifices was theirs and each person has to take responsibility for the things that they do in life. Buddhism places that responsibility upon the person who takes the action. None of us can blame others for our own failures and the parent, in the above case scenario, failed to see that it was his own expectations that let him down, rather than any action on the part of a child.

I mention this because when you make the switch over to the Buddhist philosophy, you begin to learn that the quietude within you can't be gained by expecting others to respond to your actions in a set way. Give and give gladly. Don't expect thanks. Don't do it for thanks. When you start to view all of the **Rights in the Eightfold Way,** you begin to see life in a very different way.

You learn to share smiles and tender moments, but you also learn to be more understanding and happy within yourself that you have done the best that you can when faced with dilemmas. You didn't turn your back on people that needed you. You didn't hide from human responsibility and you were not so self-absorbed that you could not observe what is happening around you. With meditation and with following as far as possible the Eight Fold Way, you begin to learn that you are responsible for your own happiness and that happiness can be a permanent state of mind. Even when bad things happen, you are able to hold onto that core foundation that keeps you balanced and able to see life clearly. It is this foundation that makes you fulfilled and at peace with the world around you.

If you break down all that you have learned about Buddhism and apply it to your observation of others, you will find that it will become a very natural way for you to behave and that you will automatically respond in a way that shows that you have taken on the values of Buddhism and incorporated them into your life with little difficulty at all and that they have enriched your life. It's all about being happy and passing that happiness on to others and observation can be a very useful tool when you are doing this because it helps you to see things from a Buddhist perspective and make more sense of the Eightfold way of Buddhism.

That's when you know it's the right philosophy for you because it makes your world a very positive world to live in and makes people around you happier as well.

Chapter 13 – More Than a Religion

"No one saves us but ourselves. No one can and no one may. We ourselves must walk the path."

~ Buddha

Can an atheist gain from Buddhist teachings? Any man or woman on Earth can gain from the teachings because they don't have to be based on religion to make sense. The Buddhist eight fold path was what came out of the meditation of Siddhartha Gautama's quest to find what could take away the suffering of mankind. He wasn't looking for solutions that only fit one particular type of person. He wasn't looking for answers for Catholics, Christians, Muslims, Hindu or for the people of any other religion. What he sought was a solution for mankind, based on the suffering that he had encountered and which disturbed him greatly.

He didn't want people to suffer any more than any living thing. In fact, such was the torment of Siddhartha that any creature on Earth suffering at all troubled him. It wasn't a question of the status of something. It was the fact that Siddhartha was looking for a solution for everyone in his philosophical way, rather than attaching his beliefs to any kind of religious order.

People don't understand sometimes that you can be very spiritual indeed, but may not have a specific belief. They see Buddhism as a religion and therefore feel that they cannot practice it because their own religion gets in the way, or that because they have no belief, they cannot encompass the ways of Buddhism into their lives, which is of course nonsense.

You don't have to have a God to be able to practice Buddhist ways. In fact, the center of your universe is actually who you are and depends upon the path that you take through your life. If you look at the opening quotation by Buddha, you will see that by walking the path, we can save ourselves from suffering and that means everyone. It takes a little while to get your head around it but I have tried to break it up into basics so that you can see that Buddhism is for everyone.

The meditation that you do helps you to strive for peace within yourself. Obviously, if you can switch off your mind and learn inner harmony, you will be happier, but it goes further than that. While you are learning Buddhist practices such as mindfulness and meditation, you are allowing your subconscious mind to work and to help you in solving the problems that you have in life.

Thus, life becomes simpler and problems become less. In the same way, if you can separate your path in life from religion itself, you can see that it can work for anyone who wants to embrace that lifestyle. When I first started looking into Buddhism, I had the same skepticism as anyone else did. I couldn't still my mind because it was conditioned to be busy. I could not practice mindfulness because I didn't know what stimulus was good for me and which was harmful. I didn't know that when you drop anger, greed, jealousy and all the other negative traits that humans embrace, you actually become a better person and life becomes much easier.

I used to judge people based on what I saw and how I was conditioned to accept what was considered as "normal." That's the problem that we all have at some stage in our lives but when you can get beyond that by practicing mindfulness and meditation, you discipline your mind to see beyond what is actually there and learn to relate to it in a way that doesn't harm you or who you are. Instead of being hyper critical, you begin to feel empathy. It doesn't make you anyone other than who you are and it doesn't change your religious beliefs, but what it does is pure magic. It makes you aware of your own fragility and keeps you grounded in everything that you do because this moment is never going to present itself as an opportunity again.

Now, when I see fault in others, I know that I have to work harder so that I see beyond that fault. I am no longer critical of people because I am only responsible for the way in which I behave and react and once that is controlled, happiness is something that comes as a benefit of learning self-discipline. I would say that Buddhism is very disciplined. You cannot try to meditate and actually gain from it unless you are prepared to work at it. Although this does not require physical work, the mental work involved in meditation is well worth it and Buddhist monks strive for perfection because they know that eventually, when you overcome all of the obstacles, you have a chance of reaching that perfect understanding which is known as "Nirvana" and following in the footsteps of Siddhartha Gautama.

Thus, meditation is important and should be taken seriously. Mindfulness is equally important because it alters your view of life and makes you much more present in this moment in time, which is what people fight. They are too busy thinking of other things to actually embrace the passing of a moment and that's a huge mistake because that moment may be all that they have.

The parts of Buddhism that you put together are shown clearly in Chapter 11 and if you go over these instances time and again, you will find that your actions and your speech, your job and your intentions all fall in with Buddhist philosophy and that it isn't a question at all of what religion you care to follow. You can believe in and act upon Buddhist fundamentals and still follow whatever religion you care to follow and that's what separates Buddhism from other religious practices since it condemns no other faith and has respect for people of different upbringings and races because that isn't the issue. The issue is how you incorporate Buddhism into the way that you behave toward others and toward yourself. It's about finding a happy medium and with the Buddhist route, you are much more likely to find it and to have it to hold onto all the way through your life.

Chapter 14 – Past, Present and Future

"Remember that silence is sometimes the best answer"

~ Dalai Lama

When you get your head around the Buddhist philosophy, you begin to see clearly how simple it is and yet how beyond the grasp of many it has become over the years. People make their lives complex. They play with emotions. They get lost in worry about the future or live with guilt from the past. Buddhism puts you into the now in a way that I can't explain any other way. Let's take a look and try to put it in laymen's terms, so that you can strive to be in that place where happiness is found.

Something bad happened in your past. For some reason, you hold onto it – perhaps as a lesson not to do the same thing again – perhaps as an emotional wound to try and protect yourself. The point is that it was in the past. You need to practice something very fundamental to get the most out of the Buddhist philosophy.

- You cannot change the past
- You cannot live in tomorrow
- All that you have is this moment

The past is gone, the future is not here yet. The moment that you are living in counts for everything. It's now. It's this actual moment and when you think about past or future, that moment is wasted and gone and served no purpose. Look at the quotation at the top of this chapter and you will see that the Dalai Lama suggests that silence is sometimes a good answer. What he means is that if you are present in this moment, regardless of whether you are with people or alone, reflective thought within this moment works very well to help you toward the next moment. Thus, meditation and mindfulness come in. Let's take my own moment and show you what I mean.

I could:

- Be concerned that the coal man is about to call and wait in the kitchen.
- I could worry about the phone call I should be making to my mother.
- I could think about something nasty that someone said to me last week.
- I could close my eyes and meditate
- I could write a poem of my thoughts in this moment
- I could make an effort to be kind to someone
- I could worry about paying a bill on time so I don't get extra charges
- I could scrub the carpet
- I would wash the car

Let's analyze these things a little further to find out which of them would be moves that would contribute toward my own happiness in this moment. The first one is future, so it doesn't apply and should be dismissed. The second one hasn't happened yet, so it is also future, unless I decide to simply stop thinking about it and do it. The third is pointless. It's going back to something that is historical, and evokes negative emotional thought. Closing my eyes and meditating could be a positive thing to do, provided that my state of mind was ready to do this. Writing a poem is devoting myself to this moment in time, so that's fine too. Being kind to someone should be something that is spontaneous, rather than connived. Worrying about a bill will serve no purpose, except perhaps saving a little money – but it's not important enough to have priority in this very moment in time. Scrubbing the carpet is positive and will give me pleasing results. Washing the car may also give me positive results. You can see that with all the choices I have, there are those that extend beyond the moment in time and that are unnecessary and I have marked these in red.

In your lifetime, you need to learn the discipline behind Buddhism if you want to embrace that as part of your life and this discipline is to take each moment and make it a positive one. Thus, doing something in the NOW is all important. As an exercise to finish this chapter, I want you to get up off your chair and do something positive, showing that you respect this moment in time and are disciplined enough mentally to put aside procrastination and do it. The more you are able to do this, the more you are encompassing the Buddhist discipline into your life. You are learning to enjoy your life and to celebrate each moment that passes. You are also learning to drop thoughts of past and future and concentrate on this moment in time. That means you are incorporating mindfulness into your life. Being mindful, you don't plan it forward or think it backwards. You live in this moment and YOU ARE that moment. That's when you understand the richness of your life and begin to get more from it than you ever have before.

Conclusion

If you were curious about Buddhism, it would pay you to watch some videos on YouTube that feature the Dalai Lama as watching the way that he behaves and the way he is disciplined is a real inspiration. For me, the Dalai Lama is a man who has discovered happiness. He is a man who spreads happiness and peace and any member of the human race can achieve that. They may never become famous or of any great significance to mankind, but that doesn't matter. The significance that they have toward others and toward themselves is what it really boils down to.

Karma is something to think about too and this means that you gain from what you reap or you get paid back for things that you do wrong. If you kill a creature, bad karma will mean that at some time, you will have bad things happen to you. If you do something that causes harm to someone else, you also have this karmic debt to pay and all men do pay this at some time in their lives. However, if you choose to live to the disciplines of Buddhism, it opens your mind to new things – helps you to feel closer to your inner self and also to the world in which you live.

Small things get put into perspective and don't grow into big things. You begin to make sense of life and want to put in the best effort that you can. Even for people with strict religious beliefs, Buddhism allows development of understanding and will make you a better Christian, a better Hindu, a better atheist or a better person because the disciplines are all about living your life to the full, without suffering unhappiness and distress. When you are able to do that, the joy that you spread to the world around you and the respect you give to yourself are one and the same. That's when you know you have found something of deep value – something that Siddhartha Gautama found 2500 years ago and wanted to share with the human race.

Bonus

Happiness and Peace are goals people spend their whole lives trying to obtain. Hopefully this book guided you in the right direction. So if you enjoyed this book, or even if you did not, I would **GREATLY** appreciate it if you could leave an honest review! Your feedback means a lot as I would like to make sure this book provides tremendous value to your life and others!

Thank you!

If you enjoyed this book and would like to get notified of FREE E-books, Upcoming releases, and get other exclusive content, join the official Xcension Publishing Book Club! You can visit http://www.xcensionpublishing.com/book-club to join!

As promised, here is your free downloadable E-book on Happiness! Just visit the website below to download it!

http://www.xcensionpublishing.com/Happiness-ebook.pdf

Made in the USA
Coppell, TX
27 March 2020